SO-AGX-762

ISBN 0-87666-834-1

Distributed in the UNITED STATES by T.F.H. Publications, Inc., 211 West
Sylvania Avenue, Neptune City, NJ 07753; in CANADA by H & L Pet Supplies
Inc., 27 Kingston Crescent, Kitchener, Ontario N2B 2T6; Rolf C. Hagen Ltd.,
3225 Sartelon Street, Montreal 382 Quebec; in ENGLAND by T.F.H. (Great
Britain) Ltd., 11 Ormside Way, Holmethorpe Industrial Estate, Redhill, Sur-
rey RH1 2PX; in AUSTRALIA AND THE SOUTH PACIFIC by Pet Imports Pty.
Ltd., Box 149, Brookvale 2100 N.S.W., Australia; in NEW ZEALAND by Ross
Haines & Son, Ltd., 18 Monmouth Street, Grey Lynn, Auckland 2 New
Zealand; in SINGAPORE AND MALAYSIA by MPH Distributors Pte., 71-77
Stamford Road, Singapore 0617; in the PHILIPPINES by Bio-Research, 5
Lippay Street, San Lorenzo Village, Makati, Rizal; in SOUTH AFRICA by
Multipet Pty. Ltd., 30 Turners Avenue, Durban 4001. Published by T.F.H.
Publications Inc., Ltd., the British Crown Colony of Hong Kong.

# Blue-Fronted Amazon Parrots

### DR. EDWARD J. MULAWKA

Gentleness is one of the characteristics often attributed to blue-fronts.

*Facing page:* Jean Broadhead of Huntington Beach, California, with two blue-fronts appropriately named Sugar and Spice.

*For permission to photograph some of the parrots shown in these pages the editors wish to thank Leo McLaughlin of Red Bank, New Jersey, and Gary Neuwirth and Susan Maione of Fins and Feathers Pet Shop, Red Bank, New Jersey.*

*Endpapers and frontis:*
Blue-fronted Amazons, *Amazona aestiva.*

**Photography:** Herbert R. Axelrod, 15, 22, 103. Tom Caravaglia, 26. Irwin Huff, 19. Ralph Kaehler, 31. Harry V. Lacey, frontis. John Moore, 83. Edward J. Mulawka, back cover, 7, 10, 11, 14, 18, 27, 58, 60, 67, 70, 71, 75, 78, 81, 82, 87, 90, 92, 96, 98, 99, 106, 110, 111. William C. Satterfield, 114, 115, 118, 119, 122, 123. David Schuelke, front cover, 16, 54, 55, 97, 102. Vince Serbin, endpapers, 23, 30, 33, 38, 46, 49, 53, 56, 66, 76, 84, 85, 94, 95, 107, 112. Louise van der Meid, 74. Courtesy of Vogelpark Walsrode, 79.

# Contents

One of the author's favorite pets is shown on these pages: a blue-front called Pow Pow, who has a vocabulary of over 250 words and expressions. Pow Pow belongs to the subspecies *Amazona aestiva aestiva*, which is the form usually found as a cage bird in the United States.

*Dedication*

To my parents, John and Frances Mulawka, whose love
and understanding have always been my staff in life.

E.J.M.

## Acknowledgments

The author is indebted to a wide variety of people who were of great assistance in making possible the final completion of this book. While they are far too many to acknowledge individually, I wish to express my gratitude for the assistance provided me by the highly competent librarians at the University of California in both Los Angeles and Irvine and by the librarians at the Los Angeles County Museum. They were most helpful in assisting me in tracking down specific accounts, even when such accounts had been referred to in the most vague of terms by earlier students of ornithology and aviculture.

I also wish to thank the numerous individuals and businesses who permitted me access to their premises and birds in order that photographs could be taken. I particularly wish to express my gratitude to the David Schuelke family of Garden Grove, California, who permitted me to photograph part of the Schuelke collection of parrots. It is always a pleasure to visit with the Schuelkes and their parrot collection, and I highly esteem their friendship. I am also indebted to Randy Hayes of Pets-a-Lot Pet Shop in Huntington Beach, California. Mr. Hayes was extremely helpful in taking time from his busy schedule to assist me in photographing some fine specimens of blue-fronted Amazons.

A blue-front shares an enclosure with a double yellow-headed Amazon, *Amazona ochrocephala oratrix (above).* Different Amazons are often housed together in zoological exhibits like this one. The double yellow head, like Pow Pow on the facing page, exhibits a behavioral characteristic common to all Amazons: the frequency with which they ruffle their feathers, particularly those of the neck. Science is uncertain as to the reasons for this behavior. It has been suggested that it makes the bird appear larger and is a warning gesture when the bird feels threatened. But behavior in captivity does not appear to bear this speculation out. Very tame birds like Pow Pow will behave thus when it is quite obvious that they are contented, happy and under no duress.

The author having a tete-a-tete exchange with Pow Pow.

# Introduction

There are about three hundred and thirty-two extant species of parrots living today. This book is concerned with only one of the three species considered to be the best talkers of them all. The three species are *Amazona ochrocephala,* the nine subspecies of which are more commonly called yellow-headed Amazons in the United States and yellow-fronted Amazons in other areas; *Psittacus erithacus,* the three subspecies of which are more commonly known as African greys; and *Amazona aestiva,* the two subspecies of which are commonly called blue-fronted Amazons or blue-fronts. These three species total fourteen separate races of parrots. While numerous other parrot species produce individuals which will mimic, usually when one is exposed to a talking parrot, hears or reads of one, it is almost invariably one of these fourteen races.

The yellow-fronts, greys and blue-fronts have been popular household pets for decades and in some cases, as with the greys, for centuries. Yet while these three species have entertained generations of children and adults and have been the object of considerable field investigations and avicultural interest, there is little information on them. It is difficult with what is presently known to establish a detailed profile of the reproduction, developmental stages and behavior of these species, whether in the wild or in captivity.

Any attempt to develop a systematic and detailed profile of any given species of parrot is—as is generally true of all

Information about captive blue-fronts (*above*), as reported by aviculturists, is likely to supplement in important respects the data about the behavior of the species in the wild. Most field studies rarely report observing the parrots from close range, either feeding or resting in trees. Being timid as they are, blue-fronts flee at the slightest provocation, so that most reports are simply sightings of birds in flight. Even if the birds were less timid, it would be difficult to observe them in the kinds of trees they frequent. The specimen shown on the facing page, one of the Schuelke collection, was photographed in a plum tree. Note how its coloration blends perfectly with the foliage.

attempts to define the various life forms which populate the world, especially wild life—contingent on a wide variety of factors. At this juncture of man's history in refining his sciences, what is known about most species of life has only resulted because of painstaking, elaborate and persistent study. However, what information is known is usually sparse, generalized and inadequate at best. What we know about parrots in general and about the species of our concern here is meager at best.

Organized life sciences, of course, have made significant progress in some areas of interest. We need only think of the progress made in agriculture and animal husbandry. After countless generations of human history, concentrated effort and experimentation have resulted in the detailed understanding of genetics, growth patterns and behavior of the various life forms essential to man's subsistence. Our understanding of the mechanics of these life forms is so thorough that we are able to manipulate both the genetic structures and environmental conditions in such ways as to minimize the effort and uncertainty of production while simultaneously increasing the yield.

Most wild forms of life are, however, basically unessential to man's survival and have never received this concentrated scientific effort, so that what we currently know about parrots is grossly limited. Yet there is still an attempt to adequately understand them.

The reasons man still does not totally understand what constitutes the characteristics and behavior of the blue-fronted Amazon *(Amazona aestiva)*, as with most others, are in part related to the species members themselves. In the wilds of their native lands, instincts govern their behavior. They are "free wheeling" agents that respond to their environment specifically according to behavioral patterns governed by instincts and, to a degree, by maturity and experience. Some parrot species, for example, nest in only the highest of trees, some of them forty meters high, making it almost impossible for men to observe the details of nesting, brooding, feeding, growth and similar life concerns related to the species. Hence, field naturalists and ornithologists generally learn nothing but the most peripheral of behavioral characteristics of the species. Further, because some species will often abandon the nest if it has been disturbed—even by so much as a simple intrusion to look in order to count the eggs—aviculturists are most reluctant to periodically investigate the contents of a nest as a procedure of scientific inquiry in order to better understand the species.

While the aviculturist can be of invaluable assistance in resolving many of the mysteries surrounding the life cycle of various species of parrots, such understandings themselves present dilemmas. For example, is the nesting behavior of a captive pair of parrots the same as what could be expected and what would be found in the wild? The caged birds live in an artificial environment controlled by the aviculturist. The birds do not have the freedom to behave as instincts dictate; they must respond to their artificial environment under conditions that man has ordered. It is man who determines choice of mate, the age at which they will be bred, the type of nesting site, the foods for the nesting and then later brooding pair, and so on.

The behavior of a given species is also seriously affected by mankind's manipulation and transformation of the physical world. Because man is both capable of and insistent on altering the physical environment in order to meet his particular needs, he concurrently alters the relationship between life forms and their habitats. Conditions which at one time favored a species may no longer exist and the species must either adapt or withdraw from the changed terrain to an environment more consistent with its own needs. For example, if a species has long been noted for frequenting and feeding in only the highest of trees, but it

This particular blue-front is in exceptionally fine feather.

*Facing page:* "Poppy" is the pet blue-front of Leo McLaughlin of Red Bank, New Jersey. Poppy is thought to be slightly more than a year old.

now feeds on or near the ground because traditional feeding environments have been destroyed, which is the more accurate description of the species' normal behavior?

Similarly, there are numerous problems concerned with determining the exact extent of a species' geographic range and distribution. Most species occupy vast terrains but not always in great numbers; they are also mobile. If, for example, a species was observed to be common near a town in 1910 but fifty years later was not immediately observable during a field expedition which lasted for three weeks in that same area, does that imply that urbanization has forced the original population to retreat or does it mean that there were specimens there of the species in question but they had not been observed for one reason or another? Suppose also that there had been four field expeditions in that area over the past one hundred years but that there had never been a sighting of a specific species; since parrots are popular and are frequently transported from one area to another, they are kept in captivity in areas that might not necessarily be part of their normal range and some might escape. If the fifth field expedition observes two specimens not observed there on the preceding four expeditions, does one infer that the species' range extends to that region or does it mean that such sightings are in actuality escaped caged birds? This kind of problem is common and it occurs frequently during field expeditions, particularly when parrots are involved.

These are only some of the kinds of concerns that naturalists and ornithologists are confronted with when on field expeditions. Eventually, however, the range is more or less established and it eventually forms the basis of evaluation for future sightings.

The problems related to the identification, study and evaluation of characteristics critical to the understanding of a specific species and of establishing a comprehensive profile are often closely associated to problems inherent within ornithology itself and similarly aviculture. As a science, ornithology is a comparative infant and it is really only within this century that it has established a systematic approach as a discipline. During its earliest history as a science, however, a great deal of confusion prevailed. Data was gathered and compiled by biologists, ornithologists, lumbermen and whoever else may have been in a given area at a given time. There were few rules governing data gathering, recording and reporting. Without the historical precedent of clearly defined procedures, chaos frequently abounded. Any cursory examination of ornithology's earliest history will soon reveal that there was an abundance of field expeditions, but there was also a proliferation of names accorded species already classified by earlier field studies. If anything, the profusion of names was a direct result of inadequate and inaccurate descriptions of birds which had been sighted, described or collected. Frequently, a new species may have already been identified, classified and named, but because of the inaccuracy of reporting, subsequent sightings or collected specimens were accorded new names and ascribed to different families. Concerning the Amazons in particular, it was not until the turn of this century that an acceptable classification and naming system was agreed upon. Further, as Harrison (1970) was to recently and astutely observe,

> Names were often given after an examination of only one or two individuals from widely separated localities and further collecting may often have revealed that such subspecies intergrade with no definite divisions between them.

In addition to the profusion and confusion of labelling systems characterizing the early ornithological and avicultural literature, the serious student of avifauna is confronted with the considerable disorder that reigns as a result of haphazard subspecies identification and classifica-

Some Amazons widely kept as pets. From farthest to nearest: a red-lored Amazon *A. autumnalis salvini;* two orange-winged Amazons, *A. amazonica;* a blue-fronted Amazon, *A. aestiva,* and a mealy Amazon, *A. farinosa.* The mealy, although a rather plain-looking bird, is one of the largest Amazons and almost invariably proves to be a gentle, affectionate pet.

*Facing page:* In general, similar parrots get along well together. While both the double yellow head and the blue-front seemed to be eyeing one another closely, they proved to be quite friendly while sitting out the photo session. These are some of the parrots in the Schuelke collection.

The eclectus parrot, *Eclectus roratus,* one of the world's most beautiful parrots, is indigenous to the South Pacific region around New Guinea. It is highly prized by aviculturists.

tion of the type about which Harrison expresses concern and as a result of the disorder which plagues ornithology because of the inability of the science to accurately define what actually constitutes a subspecies. There of course has been no lack of concentrated effort to establish parameters.

The best working definition of what constitutes a subspecies is perhaps that proposed by Mayr (1963), who defined a subspecies as ". . . an aggregate of local populations of a species inhabiting a geographical subdivision of the range of the species and differing taxonomically from other populations of the species."

The problem with the definition becomes obvious at first glance: what constitutes a taxonomic difference qualifying a geographical subdivision population with subspecies status is essentially dependent on subjective interpretation. Consider, for example, the difficulties experienced in classifying the Mexican double yellow-head *(A. o. oratrix)* and the Tres Marias *(A. o. tresmariae).* In 1900, Nelson had identified the Tres Marias as a distinct subspecies. Shortly after, six years later to be exact, Count Salvadori was to write:

> Thus far *[A. o. tresmariae]* has been separated from the true *C. Levaillanti* [a name commonly used last century for the Mexican double yellow-head *A. o. oratrix*] on account of the rather light green back, more bluish green underparts, and much greater extension of yellow on the neck, especially on the underside.

Salvadori had obviously recognized that differences existed between the double yellow-head and the Tres Marias, but he proceeded to discount these differences as unimportant, for he was to conclude:

> In common with Salvin and Godman, I have examined Tresmariaes specimens, and have failed to notice any important character to distinguish them from those of Mexico. [*i.e.,* the double yellow-head].

As if such types of complications were not enough, there are three main groups of color types characteristic of *A. ochrocephala* under the present classification system of differentiation. One group has a yellow crown, the second a yellow forehead and the third a yellow nape.

In 1966, after examining yellow-crowned specimens from both eastern and western coasts of Mexico, Monroe and Howell (1966) found a significant difference in size between the two populations and therefore reclassified *A. ochrocephala* of Mexico, *oratrix,* into two subspecific groups: *oratrix* of the Atlantic coast and *magna* of the Pacific coast, *magna* being a somewhat larger parrot. (As of the date of this writing, it does not appear that this reclassification has been accepted by the ornithological community.)

Additionally, during their investigations Monroe and Howell found three separate and isolated populations of *A.*

Like most Amazons, the blue-front loves to occupy itself by playing with whatever toys may be provided it. Playthings ensure that a cage bird will maintain good emotional health. The wooden ring satisfies the urge to gnaw and helps to keep the bill trim.

*Facing page:* Blue-fronts housed in a flight for breeding enjoying the antics made possible by a hanging length of chain.

*ochrocephala* in Belize, Honduras' Islas de la Bahia and the Honduran-Nicaraguan Caribbean border regions. Two of these populations were found to be different and subsequently classified as *parvipes* and *belizensis* subspecies. (It is not clear whether the third is a subspecies as no specimens were collected.)

*A. o. parvipes,* a yellow-naped type, in addition to some minor color differences, was found to be smaller than *A. o. auropalliatia,* the yellow-nape. *Yet because of this size differential* parvipes *has been accepted as a separate race, whereas* magna *has not!*

Ornithology is not to be faulted, however. There are insufficient resources and too few skilled scientists available to conduct all of the field work and laboratory study required to resolve all of the problems that pertain to the objects of their inquiry. Plus, there are literally thousands of species of birds. Techniques, theory and continued field study will eventually become more refined and provide avenues for rapid resolution to the diversity of concerns that demand attention.

In the meantime, as in the past, most field studies are concerned with gathering as much information on as many species as possible. With limited resources and limited manpower few expeditions can afford the luxury of studying one species of avifauna for several months, the minimal amount of time needed to comprehensively understand the life history and behavior of a species. On any field expedition any and all observations of avifauna are recorded. Sometimes virtually hundreds of different species are observed, collected or measured in some way and information duly recorded, each species receiving a sentence or two, and a geographical area seldom receives more than one or two field expeditions during a decade, if that. It is not at all surprising, therefore, to research a hundred years of ornithological history to find a specific race, and even an entire species, mentioned only a handful of times.

The yellow-naped Amazon, *A. ochrocephala auropalliata,* is undeniably one of the top three talking parrots. Yellow-napes are especially prized for their gentle disposition, and this year-old youngster is no exception.

Because of all of these difficulties there is little known about the behavior of most parrots in the wild.

One would expect that aviculture could provide us with many of the kinds of details that ornithologists are unable to supply because of inadequate resources. Aviculture, however, also has built into its system numerous handicaps which inhibit the construction of accurate profiles on many of the caged birds which interest bird fanciers, ornithologists and aviculturists alike.

There are problems related to birds themselves. Many species of birds not only refuse to breed in captivity, but many also find it difficult to survive in a captive state. Our knowledge is presently so limited that we are helpless in altering such situations. Interestingly enough, too, there must be numerous bird fanciers who are so inclined to seeing an expensive parrot as a pet that they are unable to perceive it as a possible breeding bird. They are akin, I suspect, to dog owners who have become so accustomed to perceiving dogs as pets only that their furor is aroused when dogs have been used in medical experiments, even when such experiments may have a significant effect on improving human health, or to pet dog owners who become indignant because homeless dogs that have become wild and are needlessly killing local herds of deer are shot by game wardens. Such selective perception must certainly affect some owners of exotic parrots and prevent them from attempting any breeding program with their parrots.

Such concerns, however, are more speculative than factual. Of more serious concern is the fact that while there are a considerable number of excellent avicultural journals for breeder and ornithologist alike and these have been available for over a century, there is just as much of a scarcity of data on the life cycle and behavior of most cage birds as there is in the ornithological journals. *If any group of active students of avifauna are to be faulted, surely it must be the aviculturists.*

The aviculturist is functionally in an enviable position to supply detailed information concerning any species he has successfully bred in captivity or whose behavior he has studied. Since he has a captive subject for his investigations he can easily observe the mating details of the pair, the number of copulations preceding the nest preparations by the hen and/or cock, the behavior of the cock while the hen is sitting, the exact number of eggs, their exact sizes, the appearance of the chicks when hatched, brooding duration for the hen and so on. All of these details can be recorded to provide a profile of a nesting pair. Even though such a pair is captive, at least the data would provide some insight on a species' reproductive cycle.

Unfortunately, however, there are few detailed reports published in the avicultural journals. While it is true that there are countless captive species each demanding its share of publication space in the journals, it also becomes painfully apparent after only a very limited amount of research that when there is a published article about a successful breeding, there are virtually no details provided and the article is written in the most nebulous and vague manner conceivable.

One gets the impression that there is a considerable rivalry and perhaps even jealousy among breeders, particularly when it concerns so-called "hard to breed" species. In some instances when success has been achieved and the results published, there is the possibility of ridicule. Gilbert Lee, an American who proved to be an outstandingly successful breeder of the African grey since as early as 1903, consented to provide details concerning his success only after a great deal of persuasion by the editor of *Aviculture*. Mr. Lee consented to provide details after, in the words of the magazine's 1930 editor, "We were finally able to convince Mr. Lee that while the experiment seemed rather unusual, this did not mean by any means that it was impossible."

There are numerous such examples of suggested and even flagrant ridicule. Another interesting example concerns "a gentleman from Florida" who apparently raised two African greys *(Psittacus erithacus)* at a time when, it should be remembered, it was dogmatically believed by most that it was next to impossible to breed greys in captivity. The Floridian was apparently not prepared to provide any information concerning the breeding, possibly because, as was the case with Mr. Lee, he might be ridiculed. It is difficult to imagine it, but the 1943 editor of *Aviculture*, whom one would think would know better, had the following to write about the Floridian: "With him . . . it appears to have been rather a case of 'pearls before swine,' for he had no appreciation of the accomplishment of his birds." I believe the expression best suited for the kind of rivalry referred to here is "Damned if you do and damned if you don't!"

These kinds of concerns aside, most individuals who successfully breed parrots are conscientious individuals who would prefer to share their experience with others. Unfortunately, because of their own lack of observational skills, lack of discipline or time, lack of writing skills or any one of a number of other reasons, articles on successful breeding—which could immeasurably contribute to our understanding of parrots, their growth cycle, their behavior and so on—usually are written as nothing more tangible than the breeder's pleasure with his new chicks and how delightful they are as pets!

This is indeed tragic, for as the forests retreat before man's advance and the aviculturist and bird fanciers relentlessly increase their demands for more exotic birds, many species are being threatened with extinction. For every parrot that survives to reach the quarantine station in the United States, it is estimated that quite a few more die in the process of capture, transportation and guarantining. The aviculturists are in an excellent position to develop breeding programs which may indeed help to reduce the wanton waste of wildlife in their natural habitats. Such programs, however, demand a disciplined interest in detailed study and a professional dedication to share newly acquired insights and experience with others.

In short, the blatant absence of detailed information on parrots can be in part associated with the lack of skilled scientists and financial resources necessary for data-gathering in the field. If any one group is to be faulted, however, it must be the aviculturist for his lack of dedication and interest in gathering data and for sharing what little he does share with all lovers of avifauna in a shoddy, careless and generalized manner.

The author has attempted, as completely as humanly possible, to utilize what data are available in as comprehensible a fashion as possible so that every scrap of information can be usefully employed in developing a profile of the species and subspecies presented in the following pages. In some instances there was no data available so that anything which might be written would be nothing more than guesswork. Such options were avoided. In other instances large gaps appear in what is already known, but given prudence, reasonable conclusions could be drawn with some reason to believe that the conclusions would prove correct.

Any errors in the presentation of the information, any failure to include a study or article of significance and relevance because of oversight or any conclusions which are erroneous are, of course, solely the author's responsibility.

Finally, it is sincerely hoped that the incomplete profile of the species discussed in this book will motivate the countless avifauna students to accelerate their interest in pursuing and exploring every avenue which will provide greater insight on the nature of the blue-fronts.

By better understanding these birds, we will be better able to create those conditions in captivity which will be conducive to the successful breeding of these species and others so that the pressures in the wild can be relieved.

Such insight is not uncommon. It has been achieved with cockatiels, lovebirds, budgies, and a variety of other birds which have become common household pets throughout the world.

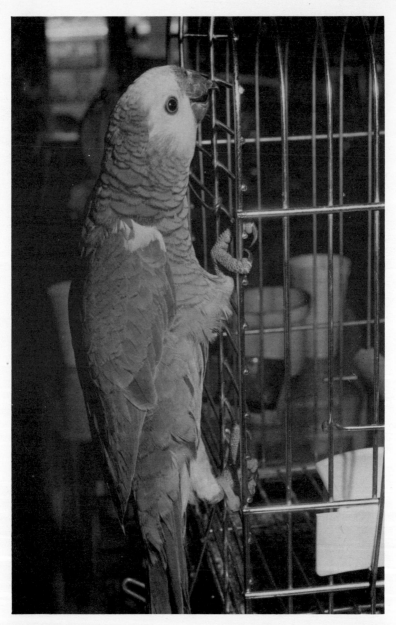

Being territorial, should parrots tire of sitting inside their cage, they will climb out and sit atop it, but rarely meander to other areas of the room. Cages for parrots are often designed so that some wires run horizontally, to facilitate climbing.

38

# General Characteristics

There are two distinct races of *Amazona aestiva*, both of them common to the central regions of South America. This species has a tendency to hybridize with other species of the genus *Amazona*, resulting in varied and pleasing color combinations which are held in high regard in Brazil. The products of such mixed breedings are referred to as "contrafeitos" and should not be confused with "races" of this species.

The two races of *Amazona aestiva* are *A. a. aestiva* and *A. a. xanthopteryx*.

## SIZE RANGES

Measurements of the wing, tail, culmen and tarsus range as follows for males of the species: wing, 214 to 242 mm; tail, 112 to 140 mm; culmen, 29 to 35 mm; tarsus, 24 to 27 mm. For females, the ranges are: wing, 199 to 229 mm; tail, 106 to 134 mm; culmen, 29 to 34 mm; tarsus, 24 to 26.5 mm.

There are no visible differences between the sexes. Females of *A. aestiva* races are generally smaller than males, but as is true with all other members of the genus *Amazona*, size cannot be employed as a sexing determinate because some females are larger than males.

The above noted sizes include both subspecies. The range of size for each race is given under that subspecies' description. It will be noted that the size of both races is almost identical except in wingspan, with *xanthopteryx* having a larger wingspan than *aestiva*.

## COMMON NAMES

Both subspecies are commonly referred to as blue-fronts or blue-fronted Amazons.

## GENERAL COLOR CHARACTERISTICS

There is considerable evidence that the blue-fronted Amazon breeds freely with other members of the genus *Amazona*. In Europe, *Amazona aestiva* has been known to breed with the white-fronted Amazon, *Amazona albifrons*, with the green-cheeked Amazon, *Amazona viridigenalis* (Hopkinson, 1939) and with the yellow-cheeked Amazon, *Amazona autumnalis autumnalis (Avicultural Magazine*, 1952-3, p. 176). There are probably other mixed matings whose results either have not been published or whose published reports are currently unknown to this writer.

Given the fact that the species will breed in captivity with other species of the genus *Amazona*, there is no reason to believe that such breedings have not occurred in the wilds. Such hybridizations no doubt primarily occur when for some reason, such as when an *aestiva* escapes into a region where its species is rare or unknown, no suitable mate within its own species is available. These interspecies matings, either in captivity or in the wild, are by no means rare events. As early as 1881, the offspring of such breedings were already recognized as common occurrences, were considered highly desirable and were popularly called "contrafeitos" in Brazil (Forbes). The blue-fronted Amazon is the most popular cage bird in that country and because of its attractive plumage, mixed matings with other species have a tendency to result in attractive and striking color combinations. These contrafeitos are highly sought after.

The blue-fronted Amazon, oddly enough, is sometimes confused with the orange-winged Amazon *(Amazona amazonica amazonica)*. This confusion can be avoided by simply remembering that the blue-front has a turquoise blue swath across the lower forehead.

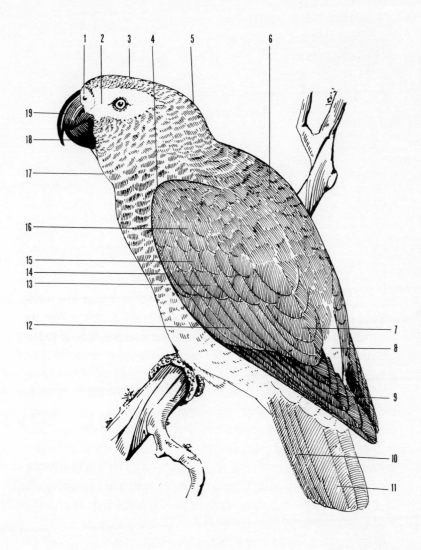

Topography of a parrot: *1*, cere; *2*, lores; *3*, crown; *4*, bend of wing; *5*, nape; *6*, mantle; *7*, tertials; *8*, rump; *9*, primaries; *10*, lateral tail feathers; *11*, central tail feathers; *12*, secondaries; *13*, greater wing coverts; *14*, carpal edge of the wing; *15*, median wing coverts; *16*, lesser wing coverts; *17*, throat; *18*, lower mandible; *19*, upper mandible.

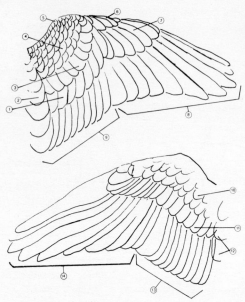

Parts of the wing.
Upper side:
1, secondary coverts
2, tertials
3, median wing coverts
4, lesser wing coverts
5, bend of the wing
6, carpal edge
7, primary coverts
8, primaries
9, secondaries
Under side:
10, lesser under-
     wing coverts
11, greater under-
     wing coverts
12, axillaries
13, secondaries
14, primaries

HEAD COLORATION: *A. aestiva* has a blue swath stretching across the forehead reaching down on both sides of the head to include the lores and in a more or less narrow strip down the side of the cheek to the edge of the upper mandible. This bluish band is more distinctly green-toned, bordering on green, and in color and size may differ from one individual bird to another. The band is separated from the periophthalmic region by a bright lemon-yellow area which begins where the blue ends and covers the crown as far back as the anterior region of the occiput and downward to include the ear coverts and chin. The upper throat may also have some yellow to it.

The remainder of the head is a parrot green.

The periophthalmic region is bare white skin. The eyelid is edged in brown-black. The iris is burnt orange with the pupil a dark brown and very prominent because of its size.

The beak is a slate black with the upper part of the upper mandible grayish shaded.

BODY: The back feathers are parrot green tinged with black. The breast feathers are distinctly lighter toned with a yellow cast to them which becomes lighter toward the upper abdominal area. Web edges on all head, back and breast feathers are edged in black at the extreme distal end giving the pattern a scalloped appearance.

WINGS: The bend of the wing is primarily yellow, but red may be interspersed throughout the bend and with some individuals the red can be the predominate color. This coloration is extensive compared to other Amazons. This color band at the wing stretches to the body. The carpal edge is a light shade of greenish yellow.

The upper wing coverts are a darker parrot green, as is true for the color wherever it may appear on the primaries and secondaries. This coloration is identical to the back coloration. The distal portion of the primaries is a violet slate shade, but the basal portion is green. The inner webs of the primaries are bluish green and the extreme outer edges of the webs are tinged with yellowish green.

The first five secondaries are poppy red on the outer webs and violet blue on the inner webs. The under coverts are a bright yellowish green. The upper covert webs are edged in black in the distal portion.

Some primaries and secondaries may also be flecked with yellow on their distal portions.

TAIL: The inner webs of the four outer tail feathers on each side are a dull red shading into a narrow band of yellow in the intermediate zone. A band of dark green straddles the remaining intermediate region, becoming a light shade of greenish yellow at the distal end of the feather. The inner webs are tinged, upon close inspection, with a dark green along the edge.

The outer webs of the extreme four tail feathers on each side are dark green in both the basal and intermediate regions and a light greenish yellow in the distal region.

When the tail is held tightly closed, the red may still easi-

Map of the geographical distribution of
the subspecies of *Amazona aestiva.*

ly be seen from both top and bottom perspectives. When the tail is fanned, a red spectrum is prominent.

The upper tail coverts are bright yellowish green. The under tail coverts are more yellowish green toned, the yellow being predominate.

FEET: The inner thighs are yellow while the outer thigh feathers are a light green color. There may be some red flecks in the "booties" of mature birds. The feet are grayish buff in color.

IMMATURES: When leaving the nest, immatures are almost identical in coloration to their parents so that, except for the eyes, it is difficult to separate the young from the old. While young blue-fronts may have less yellow or blue coverage as compared to adults, the amount of coloration on the head cannot be used as a criterion for determining age because there can be some deviation between one adult and another in the amount of head coloration.

The prominent feature of all immature birds is their dark brown eyes. The brown is so intense in both iris and pupil that it is only under very close inspection that the pupil can be discerned.

## GEOGRAPHICAL DISTRIBUTION

*Amazona aestiva* enjoys an extensive range which covers a significant portion of South America. Its most northerly range is the southern portions of Brazil's state of Piaui in the northeast. The territory encompasses all the terrain south of Piaui southward to the states of Sao Paulo and Parana.

Westward the species stretches through Paraguay, northern Argentina as far as the Andes and northward into northeastern Brazil. While the species does not include the great jungle areas of western Brazil, its range does extend throughout the states of Mato Grosso and Goias.

Blue-fronts fare best when their accommodations are commodious.

# Behavior in the Wild

*A. aestiva* is a common resident in much of the territory that it inhabits. While the terrain provides considerable opportunity to view a wide assortment of diverse avifauna co-existing in the area inhabited by the blue-front, some of them more conspicuous than others, travellers rarely fail to take note of *A. aestiva*. The bird's flight can only be described as shrieking, noisy and loud. Grante (1911) described this vocal activity as "screaming their loudest," and Kerr (1892) described this vocalization as ". . . their cries resound in all directions . . . the syllable 'caa' uttered in a great variety of inflections, and often amusingly expressive of fright, indignation, and remonstrance, according to the circumstance." Actually, it is the rare report which does not make mention of the loud screaming of the species in flight. While vocal activity is common to all Amazons in flight, the blue-front appears to be particularly more vocal than other species.

Interestingly, while feeding they appear uncharacteristically quiet and shy, assuming a degree of tameness which permits the observer to approach closely without the parrots becoming alarmed. Indeed, they are so quiet that the only evidence of their presence is the munching sounds of eating and the noise of food debris striking the ground. An interesting account of a hoped-for encounter with the blue-front during its quieter and more tame period during feeding was written by Forbes, who travelled throughout northeastern Brazil for eleven weeks in 1881. He wrote:

With the aid of my 'Gacador', Antonio, we succeeded, after a long hunt, in finding a lofty tree where the parrots were feeding, as evidenced by the heaps of its 'shelled' fruit that lay on the ground below, or came pattering down from above as we stood beneath the trees. Hoping to get a good view of some parrots at home, I proceeded to lie down on my back beneath the trees, in order to have a good look at the birds through my glasses. However, they saw us before we could 'spot' them, hidden as they were by the thick canopy of leaves, and flew screaming off to some less disturbed spot, no doubt to resume their meal on some other tree.

It is perhaps because of this exceptionally quiet behavior while in the trees that the species is generally able to escape notice and is therefore only reported being observed flying.

While there is at least one report of the species congregating in large flocks, in one instance numbering several hundred (Lonnberg, 1903), the blue-front prefers small groups in preference to large congregations. The groups usually vary in size from a pair to six or eight individuals (Grante, 1911). Sometimes a pair may have an unattached individual accompanying them (Eisentraut, 1935), perhaps an immature bird.

Regardless of flock size, however, the individuals within the group are almost always paired, each individual flying in close proximity to its partner. It is not clear whether such pairs are of the same sex or are mated pairs and, if mated, whether or not such relationships are continuous. The pairs are not spontaneous relationships, however, for the individual birds can be seen paired in the tops of trees; when frightened, they depart as a pair, even when in flocks.

At times several small flocks may be observed in the same area, but each flock is independent and apparently unrelated to the others. They have also been observed

The blue-front is one of the most attractive species in the genus *Amazona*.

(Stone and Roberts, 1931) in the immediate vicinity of orange-winged Amazons *(Amazona amazonica)*, again, though, in an independent and unrelated relationship with the other species.

As is true of most other birds, *Amazona aestiva* is a creature of habit. It has been observed to not only use the same flights from day to day, but Eisentraut (1935) found that it used separate routes to and from its roosting and feeding areas, with each route being used consistently. In flying to either roosting or feeding grounds, the flight is well above the trees, rapid and swift, and always accompanied by a "deafening noise" (Lonnberg, 1903).

At the feeding grounds small groups of blue-fronts congregate in tree crowns. Just as at other times, different flocks of feeding birds remain indifferent and separated from each other at the feeding grounds even though they may be in full and close view of each other. While the species shows a partiality for palm nuts (Wetmore, 1926), it equally searches out various fruits, seeds, nuts, berries and vegetation. While Short (1975) argues that *A. aestiva* feeds "entirely in trees," Stager (1961) found that the species was common in cultivated areas, and while he did not report them attacking crops, Pinto (1946) found them raiding crops in the state of Sao Paulo.

The species spends most of the day in the tree crowns either feeding or resting. The blue-front seems equally comfortable in both wet and dry forested areas. Additionally it seems to adapt somewhat to cultivated areas, but excessive cultivation and the concentration of large numbers of people in a region have had their effect on populations of *A. aestiva*. Pinto (1946) observed that while the species was common in the forested regions of Sao Paulo, once the great forests had been cleared and the land put under cultivation the species was no longer abundant in the region. Forshaw (1977) believes, however, that even though its status may be adversely affected in various regions, it is still common throughout its range. It might be added in this connection that it has long been noted that the blue-fronted Amazon is an extremely popular cage bird; its decrease in numbers in various localities may not be so much a result of loss of adequate cover and feeding grounds as it may be by over-harvesting the species for the pet trade.

# Behavior in Captivity

There is no question that the blue-fronted Amazon is a highly prized cage bird, not only in its native lands—as Stager (1961) explained, "... every family seems to have at least one in captivity"—but also in Europe where it has been a perennial favorite for well over a century. The harvesting and trade of the species to meet the international demand for the blue-front have been both constant and persistent. In 1881, while Forbes was in the northeastern regions of Brazil and was travelling much of the time on river boats, he noted that there were as many parrots aboard the ship as "slaves," approximately 200, with most of the parrots being blue-fronts. Just as with Stager's 1961 report, Forbes also observed almost 100 years before that most shops had dozens for sale and that "nearly every hut in the country has also its 'Papagaio'." Forbes was in Brazil in 1880 or 1881, and while it is understandable that the species was popular in its native land, the blue-front was already a popular species in Europe a century before Forbes' time, for as Greene was to write during the 1880's: "[it was] so well known that Bechstein, writing towards the close of the last century could say of it: 'This species is imported in so great numbers that it is found at every bird-seller's, and is one of the cheapest'."

There are a variety of reasons for the continued two-century popularity of the species. The main reason why they are preferred above all others is their gentleness. Like the African grey *(Psittacus erithacus)*, the blue-front is a shy bird, but the difference is that the species, once tamed, rarely assumes the indifference that is common to the grey in its rapport with people.

Its docility is legend, as is its gentleness. A typical example of the gentleness of the species was expressed by Sandi Bluestein (1978) who, after considering several different species of parrots, finally settled on a blue-front. Her selection was somewhat complicated because her husband insisted that the new parrot had to be a quiet one. She wrote: "Oscar . . . is as gentle as a newly hatched chick. He has no idea that his beak can inflict a serious wound, much preferring to sweetly kiss. My four and one half year old son can handle and play on the carpet with him." In a similar fashion, the Countess of Essex was to write in 1935 that "I can do anything with her: tickle her, roll her on her back, pick her up anyhow—nothing annoys her if I do it." Dutton was to observe a century ago that "I find them a better tempered Parrot, as a rule, than the Grey" (Greene, 1884-7). His opinion was voiced, it might be noted, at a time when the African grey parrot was considered best of all and was even popularly called the "King Parrot."

Because of this docility they can be trusted to not bite. I have had the opportunity to tame and train many of them and I have yet to be bitten hard enough where blood has been drawn, a disposition which I cannot attribute to the African greys and yellow-heads which I have handled. Because of its shyness, the blue-front generally takes some time before it will readily accept handling without attempting to flee to the safety of the cage. Yet even as a shy and frightened bronco, the blue-front can be trusted to not bite hard in its attempts to escape. Of course there are exceptions, but as a rule the species has a gentle disposition, and once it has learned to trust handling, it is a friendly parrot.

The species proves to be a hardy pet in captivity. Similar to many other parrot types which were allowed in common practice to roam about estate woods in nineteenth century

Distracted for a while from his wooden ring, Poppy turns his attention to a ring of keys.

Britain, the blue-front normally remained outdoors the entire year and survived, displaying an adaptability and hardiness not enjoyed by less fortunate species which had their ranks thinned by Britain's winters. Even in 1946, the practice of allowing almost complete freedom to parrots was practiced by some trustworthy and hardy aviculturists and bird fanciers. Risdon (1946-47) wrote that while he had to bring his African greys indoors to protect their feet from frostbite during the winter months, his blue-fronts were unaffected by the winter's cold.

This hardiness probably accounts for the many records of their longevity in captivity. While other parrots are also said to lead magically long lives and there are some accounts testifying accordingly, there appears to be far more written about *A. aestiva's* longevity than about the others. For example, during the 1880's Dr. Greene wrote about an acquaintance of his who had had one for 67 years. In 1954,

The author with Pow Pow, his pet blue-front.

Osmand was to write in *Avicultural Magazine* of two examples of longevity. Concerning the first parrot,

> The last owner had kept the bird for 14 years and had published a note in *The Star* (1944) giving its age at that date as 87 years. Stated to have been in possession of immediate family for 42 years and in the same family before that for 37 years. Total 97 years.

The second example was of a blue-front which proved to be 98½ years old. While the last owner had had it for only 9½ years, it had been in the family for the preceding 19 years. Prior to that, the parrot had been in the possession of a lady of 80 who had received the bird as a gift when she was ten years old. The last owner was finally obliged to "subject the bird to euthanasia on account of its progressive weakness and loss of appetite." That particular blue-front, according to a post-mortem, revealed tissue and organ degeneration typical of old age.

Pow Pow is something of a ham, who will give kisses when asked to "give me a kiss."

In characteristic blue-front fashion, Poppy would prefer to sit atop his cage, rather than within. While the size of this cage is sufficient for the bird's needs, enclosures less restrictive in size are preferable.

The blue-fronted Amazon is probably most admired, however, because of its speaking prowess. It is not at all unusual for the species to begin talking shortly after its acquisition. A typical example of the rapidity of learning which the species has is a two-year-old bronco blue-front which I had acquired for an acquaintance who, without seeing the parrot, decided to purchase a Moluccan cockatoo *(Cacatua moluccensis)* instead. While still untamed and untrained, that particular blue-front, eventually named Pow-Pow because of his pleasure at saying it so frequently, began saying "Hello" in the first week and three weeks later had acquired several more words. It should be emphasized that Pow-Pow did not receive any more rigorous training than a few repetitions of a word or phrase, and Pow-Pow is not a unique individual.

The species as a whole learns easily, and generally a large vocabulary is acquired. Bluestein (1978) described her Oscar as a bird whose "vocabulary is extensive, and he virtually picks up every word he hears. Whistles are his forte." Maud Knobel (1942), an active bird lover and aviculturist, acquired a young blue-front who was about three months old and wild; he said his first word approximately three weeks later and within a short time had acquired several words, whistles and songs.

The ease with which they often learn can frequently lead to interesting speculations about the bird's particular past. Pow-Pow, mentioned above, was apparently near children who played some type of war game, as children quite often do, for he enjoys neighing like a horse and then following his neighing with the pow-pow noises children would make to imitate guns. Where he learned these children's imitative war noises is a mystery. Similarly, Edward Boosey (1939), who was the first to breed the species in captivity in England, had the following speculation to make about some of their mimicry:

A blue-front given the opportunity to express its individuality is a curious and playful being. This one will play for hours on the ropes dangling from its hanging cage, thereby maintaining good emotional health.

They [ the young fledglings ] are also, I think, starting to join their parents' morning and evening chorus, which consists of the strange jumble of cries which most Amazons utter at times, supplemented, in the case of the cock, by a realistic imitation of a child being beaten by a cruel parent.

The latter is almost too realistic, particularly the gradual crescendo of screams as the child sees its wicked father approaching with the dreaded belt! I have no idea where he picked this up, but doubtless, like most of the Parrots . . . he has a fairly long and varied career behind him, spent, apparently, in a variety of households.

The blue-front is generally not a "screamer" as many other species of Amazons tend to be, even after tamed. Yet, in spite of its outstanding qualities—its gentleness, its easy tamability, its talkability—the species has never been a popular pet in the United States, despite the high European and South American esteem accorded it. Perhaps its popularity is somewhat dwarfed by the large numbers of *A. ochrocephala* which flood the United States each year and the reputation that the various subspecies of *A. ochrocephala* have earned for themselves as talkers. As Bates and Busenbark (1978) have written, "There are very few people in this country who fully appreciate or know of this bird's remarkable talent for mimicry and it is therefore overlooked as a suitable pet."

There are two other attractive features, however. The species has an attractive coloration, and it is inexpensive compared to most of the races of *A. ochrocephala* and *Psittacus erithacus*. While the species and its two races tend to be nervous birds, particularly when first acquired and they have not yet learned to trust humans, they are to be highly commended as pets.

It is a rare blue-front which requires exceptional care, which cannot be trusted and which does not reveal a talkative and pleasant disposition.

The entire species enjoys fruits and greens, showing a special partiality to fruits. Seeds are also enjoyed, but because the species seldom receives enough exercise in captivity, a heavy diet of seeds can cause serious health problems for the caged pet. The bird fancier is encouraged to provide his blue-fronts with a diet consisting primarily of greens and fruits and to be particularly parsimonious with the amount of seed provided the species in its daily feedings. Actually, a blue-front accustomed in captivity to a diet of greens and fruit similar to that which it would enjoy in the wild will almost always eat the seeds and nuts only when there are no more fruits or vegetables left in the food dish.

The blue-front always makes a handsome and charming pet. "Mork" enjoys his relationship with Helen Schuelke, his mistress. Though he has a large vocabulary, Mork frequently reverts to parrot babbling, as he is doing now.

# Breeding

Little is known about the blue-front's breeding and nesting behavior in the wild. They are known to nest between October and March, choosing hollows in towering palm trees (Kerr, 1892). Orfila (1938) reports that the same hollow in a palm tree was used annually by what he believed was the same nesting pair. The nest is described by Naumberg (1930) as a natural cavity in which two or three eggs are laid on the decaying wood without the benefit of any nesting materials. The Naumberg observation of clutch size appears to be an estimate, as the usual number of eggs laid per clutch is four. The eggs are white and ovate. Schonwetter (1964) reports the size of the eggs as being 36.1 to 40.8 mm by 28.0 to 30.6 mm.

Most of what is known about the breeding of *A. aestiva* comes from successful breeding results in captivity. Given the species' two-hundred-year relationship with Europe, it is surprising to find few documented successful breedings in the literature. During the 1880's Greene had written that "There are many recorded instances of these birds laying eggs in captivity, but none, with which we are acquainted, of their having produced young." Indeed, it was not until 1939 that the British Avicultural Society gave recognition to the first recognized, and officially recorded, breeding of the species.

Seth-Smith (1943) reported to the *Avicultural Magazine's* readership an article he had read concerning a Dr. Wyss who had successfully bred the blue-front in Switzerland in 1894. According to Dr. Wyss, the pair had complete freedom of the meadows and forests of Hunenberg, Switzerland, during each spring and summer for twenty years before the pair showed any interest in breeding. That year, 1894, a clutch of four was laid, hatched and successfully reared by the pair. No further details were given for that first nest.

In the following year another clutch of four was laid and successfully reared, and the results were reported in the July issue of *Feathered World.* This time a few details were provided.

The nesting site chosen was a deep hole in the trunk of an old pear tree. While Dr. Wyss reported few other details, he was careful to note that the eggs were laid with regularity every third day: June 13, 16, 19 and 22.

As has been mentioned earlier, it was common practice in Europe during the previous century to permit exotic birds full or almost complete freedom, especially during the spring and summer months, and it was usually only the more delicate species which were taken indoors during the winter months. While Dr. Wyss kept his two blue-fronts and their young indoors during the colder months, British aviculturists preferred to keep their exotics, even the more delicate species, outdoors. Given that *A. aestiva* was given this freedom and proved hardy enough in Dr. Wyss' case to rear two successful families of four, and the first family was not started until the pair was twenty years old, one would have expected to hear of more such successful captive breedings, particularly of pairs with full freedom.

The literature, however, proved silent for over forty years until Edward Boosey successfully bred a pair in 1939, the event winning Mr. Boosey an award in its recognition. Mr. Boosey, as a matter of record, was also the first to suc-

A hollow log will at times stimulate an interest in breeding.

cessfully breed the African grey *(Psittacus erithacus)* in Britain.

One suspects, however, that 19th century avicultural practices were partially based on the belief that if given absolute freedom, any type of exotic bird will freely breed in captivity. One notes in the literature that at the beginning of this century the practice of permitting parrots substantial freedom was being gradually curtailed; the birds were being placed in flights and modern animal husbandry was beginning to have its effect on aviculture.

In 1929, Tavistock, in giving the usual annual report on the status of his collection of exotic birds, reported anticipating some nesting success with blue-fronts:

The Lutino blue-fronted Amazon once more disappointed me, or rather her mate did. This cock, when introduced to her nearly two years ago, tried hard to make himself agreeable. She, however, was persistently rude to him. He never forgave her, and ultimately turned so spiteful with her that I had to keep his wing partly cut.

An attempt to resolve the unhappy situation reflects new methods being used in aviculture, practices which only a very few would have even considered forty years previously. The pair were separated for a while and later reintroduced into the same flight. The hen apparently went to considerable lengths to groom the cock, but "he would still turn on her without warning." Tavistock was finally obliged to find him a home as a cage bird. For just such a contingency Tavistock had kept a cock in reserve, but he also proved to be a disappointment because he was "a spiritless creature . . . much oppressed by the horseplay of the lively female with him." At the time of writing (1929), Tavistock did not appear too dismayed over the failures, writing optimistically, "I am promised another cock reputed to be well disposed towards matrimony."

Tavistock was not the only avid aviculturist to observe severe difficulties between cock and hen in their domestic or familial relationships. Smith (1942) reported that his pair had had four clutches over four years, each time hatching at least one chick; in each case the nestlings would be found dead within three weeks because of parental abandonment or other causes which Smith was uncertain about.

Similarly, after his initial success in 1939, Boosey continued to breed the original pair with equally successful results. However, several years later (1949) when he attempted to breed other blue-fronts, he suffered some disappointments and setbacks. He tried to encourage a successful pairing with two other blue-fronts which he had. When he placed them in a flight with a nest box they seemed to show considerable excitement at seeing the nest box, but they soon lost interest and "concentrated instead on planning the amputation of my fingers when I fed them." Mr. Boosey decided to encourage a third pair, but while the efforts to pair the birds did not put his own fingers into immediate jeopardy, it did result in the loss of his hen, for as he was to explain, "he managed to murder [the hen], scalping her savagely after they had been together for several weeks."

Needless to say, Mr. Boosey did successfully breed the blue-front, and it was only shortly after his 1939 success that Mr. Smith encountered his four years of difficulties with his pair. Smith had purchased two blue-fronts while in South America. Over the following twenty years the hen had laid several clutches before he realized they were a "pair." In 1939, he decided to let the hen sit on her clutch of four. She hatched two, which were killed either by the hen or the cock a week after hatching. He was advised to separate the pair after the next successful hatching; this he did in 1940. The one hatched chick, however, died two weeks later. In 1941, he tried another experiment: he filled the nest box with sawdust instead of the usual sand. The hen faithfully attended the eggs, hatching one chick and then abandoning it after four weeks. Smith hand-raised that one sole survivor. The year of the writing of the article (1942), the hen had again incubated another clutch, the size not reported, and eighteen days after hatching the chick died. Aside from the one effort to rescue the one chick and hand-raise it, all other successful hatchlings were lost.

Boosey's pair, however, continued nesting for several years after their first successful family in 1939, until 1950 when, according to his published account of that year, the hen laid an infertile clutch—"this time with a new husband." It should be of special interest to note that the hen had laid an annual clutch of four for ten years in a row and had successfully hatched and reared all of the young!

While blue-fronts are generally timorous creatures, they can easily be taught to accept handling. Poppy is quite adept at stepping from finger to finger, which is one of the primary taming exercises.

Randy Hayes's blue-front was a mostly untamed bird before the handling required for the photo session.

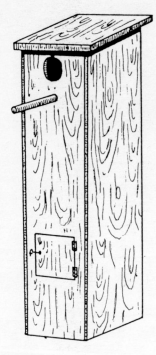

A "grandfather clock" next box. The hatch near the bottom allows nest inspection.

Boosey did not receive the pair until September 1938. He housed them in a normal parakeet flight which was 15' long, 5' wide and 7' high, and which had one-half-inch wire mesh to reinforce a larger mesh already in place. The flight, of course, was outdoors where the blue-fronts remained all winter.

When a grandfather clock nest box was introduced to the flight in March, 1939, the hen "took to it at once" and "thereafter was only very occasionally seen." Because the cock zealously defended the nest box area, Boosey had no idea how many eggs were in the clutch until the young were all hatched and the eldest of the brood was already feathering well. What Boosey did notice, however, was that the cock frequently disappeared into the nest box and would remain there for extended periods of time.

According to Smith (1942), during incubation the hen is seldom seen; she rarely leaves the nest more than once a day, and that for only a short duration. During the entire incubation period and brooding the cock attentively feeds the female.

One of the problems facing a breeder, particularly one faced with feeding a family of young birds whose species infrequently breeds in captivity and about which there is little reliable information, is the difficulty of ensuring that the parents are receiving the appropriate foods necessary for the healthy growth of the offspring. During the previous century it was established practice for British aviculturists to supply the brooding pair with bread and milk in addition to whatever seeds or fruits might at that time be in vogue in avicultural theory and practice. Even during the 1920's when it could be assumed that British aviculture had become more sophisticated, Lord Tavistock (in Boosey, 1939) continued feeding his brooding pairs bread soaked in milk as a mainstay of the daily diet.

When faced with the problem of feeding his brooding pair of blue-fronts, Boosey's feeling was that the adult birds might weary with feeding their young because traditional foods for parrots generally consisted of small seeds. Indeed, it has often been noticed that parrots sometimes abandon otherwise healthy nestlings, and there may be merit to the belief that the nestlings' demands are too much for the parents to cope with when the diet provided the adults does not facilitate the rapid conversion of solids into "milk" which is regurgitated to the young in the feeding process.

Undoubtedly, in the wild the brooding parents instinctively choose those fruits, seeds or vegetation which can be rapidly predigested and fed the youngsters as needed. If the foods are inappropriate, the digestive processes in the adult bird proceed slower while concurrently the youngsters are hungry and demanding food. The parental inability to adequately feed the young because of the inappropriateness of the food provided them could force the parents to eventually abandon the young. This is nature's way of preserving

Photographed out-of-doors, this lovely blue-front was at first somewhat bewildered and confused by the usual sounds of traffic, children playing, and what have you. But, in typical blue-front fashion, it rapidly adjusted to the unfamiliar surroundings and eventually even allowed itself to be petted.

The gentleness of this basically untamed bird indicates that it will be a good pet. Also, it was already beginning to talk.

the health and survival of the mature birds. Brooding pairs in captivity cannot instinctively choose from a variety of foods. They can only choose from that which is provided by the breeder.

Boosey's resolution to this potential problem was to follow Lord Tavistock's practice of providing the parenting pair with a supplement of bread soaked in milk. The mainstay of the pair's daily diet was, as Boosey referred to it, a "catholic diet": boiled cod, scrambled eggs and boiled potatoes (since they were the day before's leftovers, they had butter on them)! The food provided that pair of blue-fronts would certainly compete with any continental European restaurant's menu.

Boosey's observation (1939) was that the brooding pair "consumed enormous quantities" of the eggs, potatoes and cod, and they were encouraged to eat heartily of these foods because Boosey provided them with as much as they could consume. They were also given rations of hemp seed, canary, sunflower and monkey nuts.

While such a daily diet may appear to be somewhat questionable, unorthodox or even bizarre by the standards of the more conservative members of the avicultural community, it should be remembered that that same pair of blue-fronts successfully reared an annual brood of four from 1939 to 1949—all on a diet primarily consisting of potatoes (with butter), cod and scrambled eggs! For the information of persistent skeptics, Boosey was not only awarded the British Avicultural Society's highest award for breeding the blue-fronts in captivity, but he was also awarded this honor for successfully breeding the African greys *(Psittacus erithacus)*.

Unlike Smith's pair which inadequately cared for their young, Boosey's pair of blue-fronts were extremely attentive to the brood. When he was eventually unable to curb his curiosity and finally peeked into the nest, he found that, as is true of parakeets, the four offspring were all of different ages and at different stages of growth. While the oldest were quite large and "feathering" well, the youngest was still a down-covered nestling. Boosey was later to report (1939) that the youngest eventually had one of its legs bowed. While Boosey did not report the size of the nesting box, it could be accurately inferred that it was probably too small for the family of four and the bowed-leg youngster was simply being crushed by the others.

It is interesting to note the different dates provided by the various breeders who have reported some details concerning the stages of development of the young. Smith (1942) only reported one set of dates for the four clutches which were laid between 1939 and 1942. The hen started sitting on June 18th; on July 17th the chick had hatched and by the 25th its eyes were open. Apparently Smith's hen annually laid her eggs during June, for he wrote: "The time of laying the eggs occurs at the beginning of June." Boosey's breedings, also in England, provide a different set of dates. The first of the young 1939 fledglings left the nest on July 20th, the eggs being laid, as inferred by Mr. Boosey, sometime during the first week of April. Dr. Wyss' pair, it will be recalled, laid their clutch between June 13th and June 22nd, and by August 30th all of the four youngsters had left their nest (Seth-Smith, 1943).

When they leave the nest, the young fledglings' eyes are colored dark brown (Boosey, 1939); this is about the only distinguishing feature between the young birds and their parents. The eye coloration turns into the normal coloration of the adult at approximately seven months of age. Mrs. Knobel (1942) reported that her Richard's eyes turned orange so fast that "this seemed to happen in a day."

The young are for all practical purposes quite independent when they leave the nest. They are capable of flying immediately. Boosey's young blue-fronts were seen feeding themselves two days after leaving the nest (Boosey, 1939).

There have been some instances of blue-fronts in which the coloration departs from that normally found. Jerome Buteyn's blue-front (*above*) was described as having a yellowish olive color, with the blue much paler (which makes one think of the Yellow factor operative in other parrot species). In those individuals characterized as "lutinos," one supposes that all areas that are green on a normal individual (like Pow Pow on the facing page) are a yellow color instead.

Blue-fronted Amazon, *A. aestiva.*

# The Subspecies *aestiva*

## *Amazona aestiva aestiva* (Linné) 1758

*A. a. aestiva* is commonly referred to as the blue-fronted Amazon or simply blue-front. These names are also applied to *A. a. xanthopteryx* primarily because there is little difference in appearance between the two races aside from a minor size difference and a difference in the coloration of the bend of the wing.

**Physical Dimensions**

The recorded minimum and maximum dimensions of the wing, tail, culmen and tarsus of males of *A. a. aestiva* are as follows: wing, 214 to 232 mm; tail, 112 to 140 mm; culmen, 30 to 34 mm; tarsus, 24 to 27 mm.

For females, the dimensions are: wing, 199 to 218 mm; tail, 106 to 121 mm; culmen, 29 to 32 mm; tarsus, 24 to 26 mm (Forshaw, 1977).

**Sexual Differences:** None. There is a general belief that sexual differentiation can be made on size alone because the males tend to be larger than females. However, there is such an overlap in size dimensions between the two sexes that size cannot be used as an accurate measure of sexual differentiation. There is a similar belief that the color patches on the bend of the wing are indicative of sex (Boosey, 1948-49) when in fact bend of the wing coloration is an indication of the race to which the individual belongs.

Because the orange-winged Amazons, *A. amazonica,* also show blue and yellow on the head, they are often confused with blue-fronts. Notice, however, that the bill of the blue-front is completely dark, lacking the light area toward the base of the bill of the orange-wing.

Blue-fronted Amazon, *A. aestiva aestiva.* The nominate form was described by Linnaeus in 1758. If the specimen found by Berlepsch more than a century later looked like the one shown below, one can understand why he would wish to separate it as a subspecies, naming it *xanthopteryx,* "yellow-winged."

While this specimen is considered by some to be a good example of *xanthopteryx,* others would argue that the extensive yellow on the wing is not found in most other specimens that might be classified into this subspecies.

## PHYSICAL DESCRIPTION

The race interbreeds freely with *xanthopteryx* along the lines of intergradation where the two races' territories meet. Some individuals, therefore, will be difficult to identify as to the appropriate race.

Additionally, as is true of *xanthopteryx*, *aestiva* is known to breed in captivity with other species of Amazons, and no doubt such hybrids occur in the wilds.

**Head Coloration:** The most outstanding features of *aestiva's* head coloration are the turquoise blue band across the lower forehead and the bright lemon yellow covering much of the head area.

The turquoise band stretches across the lower forehead region, extending down to the lower edges of the upper mandible. Some turquoise blue flecks may often be seen on the lores and cheek area.

The yellow begins where the turquoise ends on the forehead and continues to the intermediate crown, more or less, sometimes extending as far back on the head as to the occiput. The yellow includes the cheeks, lores, ear coverts and frequently the upper throat.

The remainder of the head is parrot green with the terminal edges of the green feathers finely edged in brown-black.

The beak is a dull slate-black with the upper regions of the upper mandible a grayish shade. The iris is a burnt orange. The appearance of the eye is unforgettable because the pupil is quite large.

**Body:** The back feathers are parrot green and the breast feathers are a yellowish green. The back feathers, as with the green head plumage, are finely edged in a brown-black on the terminal ends of the feathers.

**Wings:** The upper coverts are a dark green, similar to much of the green color found on the primaries and secondaries. The distal portions of the outer webs of the primaries are a dull green and the inner webs are a violet-

Blue-fronted Amazon, *A. aestiva.*

It is often difficult to classify a particular blue-fronted Amazon into one or the other of the two subspecies. Even though a specimen may come from an area where there seems no possibility of the two subspecies interbreeding, it may show unexpected coloration on the shoulder and bend of the wing. Of the specimens shown on these pages, the one in the foreground above best conforms to the description of *A. aestiva aestiva,* while the almost completely yellow shoulders of the specimen on the facing page (belonging to Randy Hayes) characterize *A. aestiva xanthopteryx.* Further study may show that differences in the coloration of individuals is smoothly clinal—the geography of the range of the species does not preclude this possibility.

Alertness and interest in what the humans around are doing is characteristic of the pet Amazon.

Three Amazons keeping an eye on the photographer. The nearest is a green-cheek, *A. viridigenalis;* the two behind are yellow-napes, *A. ochrocephala auropalliata.*

black. The first five secondaries forming the speculum are red in the outer webs and a blue-black in the inner webs.

The under coverts are a distinct yellow green. The bend of the wing is extensively colored in red, which appears as a distinct triangular patch on the folded wing. There may be flecks of yellow, particularly on the edge.

**Tail:** The inner two feathers are a parrot green. The outer four feathers on each side have inner webs which are dark green in the intermediate areas, ending with a yellowish green in the distal portion. The outer webs are a bright poppy red in the intermediate zone, followed by a parrot green and finally at the distal portion a yellowish green.

Both inner and outer tail coverts are a bright yellowish green.

**Feet:** The inner thighs are yellow and the outer thighs a yellowish green. The feet are a brown-gray.

The blue-front above has a considerable amount of white on the forehead. A great many other individuals, however, have no white whatever. Some have a predominance of yellow to the cheeks and forehead, while others have almost no yellow whatever and are almost completely blue. The coloration of the head, however, is not a subspecific character, in the opinion of most; thus the red on the bend of the wing would place this specimen in the subspecies *aestiva.*

Of these blue-fronts, both owned by Randy Hayes, one is the *xanthopteryx* already shown. The other, some would say, is a *contrafieto,* a bird of uncertain ancestry, perhaps an interspecific hybrid. Others would maintain that its coloration is nothing more than one of the variations possible among blue-fronts.

Map of the geographical distribution of
*Amazona aestiva aestiva.*

**Immatures:** When fledged, the young *aestiva* are more or less like their parents in coloration. At approximately seven or eight months, the dark eyes assume the orange coloration of adulthood. The blue on the forehead may not be as prominent.

**Note:** The adult *aestiva* has a shorter wing span than *xanthopteryx*.

## GEOGRAPHICAL DISTRIBUTION

*A. a. aestiva* is confined to the east central regions of Brazil. Its most eastern range is in the states of Pernambuco and Paraiba (Lamm, 1948), which are on Brazil's northeastern seaboard. Westward, the race is common in the southern regions of the state of Piaui (Short, 1975). Southward the species has been found common in the states of Mato Grosso at Descalvados (Naumberg, 1930) and Chapada (Allen, 1893) and in the central region of Goias, where it has been observed as common at Chapada dos Veadoerios (Stager, 1961). Eastward, again along the eastern seaboard, the range includes the state of Sao Paulo where Pinto (1946) observed it as being common.

*A. a. aestiva* is considered a common parrot in its range, which actually encompasses approximately half of Brazil's geographical territory. The race does not reach northward anywhere in its habitation to include the Amazon River region. Its most westward boundaries do not include the western tropical forest states of Pará or Amazonas.

Frayed tail feathers are often seen on untamed, wild-caught parrots. Once the bird has a permanent home and becomes accustomed to human presence, the next molt usually remedies this unsightly condition.

*Facing page:* Illustration of the blue-fronted Amazon, which first appeared in W. T. Greene's *Parrots in Captivity* (1884-87).

Blue-fronted Amazon, *A. aestiva xanthopteryx.*

# The Subspecies *xanthopteryx*

*Amazona aestiva xanthopteryx* **(Berlepsch) 1896**

*A. a. xanthopteryx* is commonly called the blue-fronted
Amazon or blue-front.

**Physical Dimensions**

The recorded minimum and maximum dimensions of the
wing, tail, culmen and tarsus of males of *A. a. xanthopteryx*
are as follows: wing, 234 to 242 mm; tail, 123 to 135 mm;
culmen, 29 to 35 mm; tarsus, 24.5 to 27 mm.

For females, the dimensions are: wing, 221 to 229 mm;
tail, 115 to 134 mm; culmen, 29 to 34 mm; tarsus, 24 to
26.5 mm.

**Sexual Differences:** None. The race is not dimorphic.
There are no size, shape or color characteristics which can
be employed to differentiate sexes.

## PHYSICAL DESCRIPTION

There are so few differentiating characteristics between
*A. a. xanthopteryx* and *A. a. aestiva* that a complete descrip-
tive review of the physical characteristics of *xanthopteryx*
would be needless repetition. This same observation may
be applied to particulars concerning *xanthopteryx's* diet or
behavior as a caged bird and pet.

There are a few minor characteristics, however, which
will be of import to the ornithologist, bird fancier and
aviculturist.

There are two basic distinguishing differences between
*A. a. aestiva* and *A. a. xanthopteryx*. One basic difference
applies to size, whereas the second difference relates to coloration of the bend of the wing.

Although blue-fronts are somewhat shy and retiring, as compared with other kinds of parrots, their trust can generally be won, particularly if bribed with a favorite tidbit.

*Facing page:* Use of the foot to hold food while it is being consumed is common to many parrot species.

This blue-front held by Randy Hayes is between two and three years old.

The first basic difference lies primarily in the span of the wing. *A. a. xanthopteryx* has a decidedly larger wing span than *A. a. aestiva*. Additionally, both males and females tend to have longer tails than *A. a. aestiva*. Because of these slight size differences, *xanthopteryx* appears larger and tends to be somewhat heavier in weight.

The second major difference lies in the coloration of the bend of the wing. *A. a. xanthopteryx* has a *predominate* amount of yellow to the bend, even though there may be some red flecked throughout the area, particularly along the edge, whereas *A. a. aestiva* has a predominately red bend, although that too may be flecked with yellow. As with *A. a. aestiva*, the coloration is extensive, forming a clearly discernible triangle on the folded wing bend.

Another view of the author with Pow Pow.

The photos on this and the facing page were taken some months apart. Both show Pow Pow, the author's pet blue-front.

Captive breeding of the blue-fronted Amazon has shown that, unlike some other Amazons, coloration changes very little with time. By the time an individual is a year old—perhaps sooner—it will be fully colored, and the differences resulting from subsequent molts will be insignificant.

Map of the geographical distribution of
*Amazona aestiva xanthopteryx.*

# GEOGRAPHICAL DISTRIBUTION

*A. a. xanthopteryx* occupies a territorial range south and west of that occupied by *A. a. aestiva*. This race is found primarily in Bolivia, Paraguay, Argentina and the most southwestern portions of Brazil.

In Brazil the race is confined primarily to the state of Matto Grosso, where it is found to be common at Pan de Azacur (Grante, 1911); Cherrie (1916) also found it common through most of the southwestern portions of the state. The race has been recorded as common in Paraguay at Chaca Austra (Glydenstolpe, 1945) and Pinasco (Wetmore, 1926). Additionally, there have been several other sightings throughout the country.

In Argentina the subspecies is found as far west as Salta in the northwest and as far southwest as Tucuman (Salvin, 1880). Forshaw (1977) reports that the race is occasionally found as far south as the northwestern Buenos Aires region.

Along the Pacific region of the South American continent, the race extends northward into the southeastern areas of eastern Bolivia, where it has been found common at Fortin Crevaux (Glydenstolpe, 1945) and throughout the Bolivian Chaco (Eisentraut, 1935). Forshaw (1977) extends the race's most northerly boundaries into northern Bolivia. Its range appears to be restricted to areas east of the Andes.

Slow, deliberate movements are an important part of winning a parrot's trust. Gentleness on the part of the owner will be repaid by gentleness from the parrot.

*Facing page:* Forest in Brazil, an example of the vegetation found within the range of the blue-front.

# Bibliography

Allen, Joel A. "On a Collection of Birds from Chapada, Matto Grosso, Brazil, made by Mr. H.H. Smith." *Bulletin of the American Museum of Natural History,* Vol. 5, 1893, pp. 107-158.

Bates, Henry J. and Robert I. Busenbark. *Parrots and Related Birds,* T.F.H. Publications, New Jersey, 1978.

Bluestein, Sandi. "Oscar, A Blue Fronted Amazon." *American Cage-Bird Magazine,* August 1978, p.12.

Boosey, Edward. "The Breeding of Blue-Fronted Amazon Parrots for the first time in Great Britain." *Avicultural Magazine,* Vol. 4, 5th ser., 1939, pp. 393-396.

Boosey, Edward. "Breeding Results at the Keston Foreign Bird Farm, Season 1949." *Avicultural Magazine,* Vol. 56, 1950, pp. 17-20.

Boosey, Edward. "Sexing Blue-Fronted Amazons." *Avicultural Magazine,* Vol. 54-55, 1948-49, p. 113.

Cherrie, G.K. "A Contribution to the Ornithology of the Orinoco Region." *Museum of the Brooklyn Institute of Arts and Sciences Bulletin,* Vol. 2, 1916, pp. 133-374.

Editor's Note. *Aviculture,* Vol. 2, 1930, p. 257.

Eisentraut, M. "Biologische Studien im Boliviamische en Chaco, VI." *Beitrag zur Biologie der Vogelfauna,* Mitt. Zool. Mus. Berlin, 20, 1935, pp. 367-443.

Essex, Countess of. "Polly—My Amazon." *Avicultural Magazine,* Vol. 13, 4th ser., 1935, pp. 277-280.

Forbes, W. "Eleven Weeks in the North Eastern Brazil." *The Ibis,* 1881, pp. 312-362.

Forshaw, Joseph M. *Parrots of the World.* T.F.H. Publications, New Jersey, 1977.

Glydenstolpe, Nils. "A Contribution to the Ornithology of Northern Bolivia." *Klung. Vetenskapsakdemiens Handligar,* Vol. 23, 1945, pp. 1-485.

Grante, H.B. Claude. "List of Birds Collected in Argentina, Paraguay, Bolivia, and Southern Brazil, with Field Notes." *The Ibis,* 1911, pp. 317-350.

Greene, Dr. W. T. *Parrots in Captivity,* T.F.H. Publications, New Jersey, 1979. (Reprint of original text published in three parts between 1884 and 1887.)

Harrison, C.J.O. "Subspecies and Aviculture: Some Notes on Recent Difficulties." *Avicultural Magazine,* Vol. 76, 1970, pp. 191-194.

Hopkinson, Dr. (Comment by Dr. Hopkinson on the successful breeding of *Amazona aestiva* by Edward Boosey in 1939.) *Avicultural Magazine,* Vol. 4, 5th ser., 1939, p. 396.

Kerr, J. Graham. "On the Avifauna of the Lower Pilcomayo." *The Ibis,* Vol. 4, 1892, pp. 120-152.

Knobel, E. Maude. "Richard—A Young Amazon Parrot." *Avicultural Magazine,* Vol. 7, 5th ser., 1942, pp. 20-21.

Lamm, Donald W. "Notes on the Parrots of the States of Pernambuco and Paraiba, Brazil." *Auk,* Vol. 65, 1948, pp. 261-283.

Lonnberg, Dr. E. "On a Collection of Birds from Northwestern Argentina and the Bolivian Chaco." *The Ibis,* 1903, pp. 26-471.

Mayr, E. *Animal Species and Evolution.* Oxford University Press, London, 1963.

Helen Schuelke is amused by Mork's attentions.

Parrots, like many other birds, are attracted by shiny objects. Thus it's no surprise that Poppy is still worrying the ring of keys.

Monroe, B.L. and L.T. Howell. "Geographic Varieties in Middle American Parrots of the *Amazona ochrocephala* Complex." *Occasional Papers of Zoology, Louisiana State University,* #34, 1966, pp. 1-18.

Naumberg, Elsie M. "Birds of Matto Grosso, Brazil." *Bulletin of the American Museum of Natural History,* Vol. 60, 1930, pp. 1-432.

"The Nest Box." *Aviculture,* Vol. 13, 1943, p. 15.

News and Views. *Avicultural Magazine,* Vol. 58-59, 1952-53, p. 176.

Orfila, R.N. "Los Psittaformes Argentinos." *Hornero,* Vol. 6, 1938, pp. 1-21.

Osman, W.C. "Longevity in Psittacine Birds." *Avicultural Magazine,* Vol. 60, 1954, p. 165.

Pinto, O.M. "Aves Brasileiros da Familia dos Papagaios." *Relat. a. Institute Bot., Sao Paulo,* 1946, pp. 126-129.

Risdon, D.H.S. "Aviculture in the Arctic Weather." *Avicultural Magazine,* Vol. 52-53, 1946-47, pp. 86-88.

Salvadori, Count T. "Notes on the Parrots, Part IV," *The Ibis,* Vol. 48, 1906, pp. 642-659.

Salvin, O. "A List of Birds Collected by the Late Henry Durnford during his Last Expedition to Tucuman and Salta. " *The Ibis,* Vol. 22, 1880, pp. 351-364.

Schöenwetter, M. *Handbuch der Zoologie,* Academie-Verlag. bd. 1, Lief 9, Berlin. 1964.

Seth-Smith, D. "Correspondence." *Avicultural Magazine,* Vol. 8, 5th ser., 1943, p. 28.

Short, Lester L. "A Zoogeographical Analysis of the South American Chaco Avifauna." *Bulletin of the American Museum of Natural History,* Vol. 154, 1975, pp. 165-352.

Smith, G.D. "Breeding and Rearing Blue Fronted Amazon Parrots." *Avicultural Magazine,* 5th ser., 1942, pp. 149-150.

Stager, K.E. "The Machris Brazilian Expedition; Ornithology: non-passerines." *Contributions to Science, Los Angeles County Museum,* Vol. 41, 1961, pp. 1-27.

Stone, W. and H.R. Roberts. "Zoological Results of the Matto Grosso Expedition to Brazil in 1931, III, Birds." *Proceedings of the Academy of Natural Science, Philadelphia.* Vol. 86, 1935, pp. 363-397.

Tavistock. "Notes on the 1929 Breeding Season." *Avicultural Magazine,* Vol. 7, 4th ser., 1929, pp. 233-240.

Wetmore, Alex. "Observations on the Birds of Argentina, Paraguay, Uruguay, and Chile." *Bulletin of the U.S. National Museum,* Vol. 133, 1926, pp. 1-448.

*Above:* The author's pet double yellow head, named Selsa. *Facing page:* Cisco is a lilac-crowned Amazon, *A. finschi,* owned by Lindsay Salathiel of Newport Beach, California. Like the double yellow head and most other Amazons, the lilac-crowned is not sexually dimorphic.

By this time, Poppy is ready to work at extracting the peanut's kernel. Since both sexes of the blue-fronted Amazon look alike, surgical sexing is the most certain way to determine a bird's sex.

# Diagnostic Laparoscopy in Birds

*William C. Satterfield, D.V.M.*

## What is laparoscopy?

Laparoscopy is a procedure for examining the spaces within the body without major surgical invasion of those spaces. The laparoscope is an instrument developed over twenty years ago for use in human medicine. Since the late 1960's, the miniaturized laparoscope—which employs a fiberoptic system—and accompanying instruments have been used by physicians in procedures such as examination of the unborn fetus and the knee in humans. Application of the laparoscope to bird sexing came in the earliest phase of its veterinary use.

Light from a remote source of illumination travels through a small, flexible, glass-filled tubing to a viewing tip with an eyepiece. The light level is adjustable to allow the veterinarian to select the best illumination for the procedure. Most laparoscopes contain a magnification system which enlarges the final image up to thirty times, allowing close-up, detailed examination of the surface of the organs. Viewing tips are available in various sizes, but avian laparoscopy is often done with a 2.2 mm diameter (14-gauge) tip, which is about the size of a large hypodermic needle.

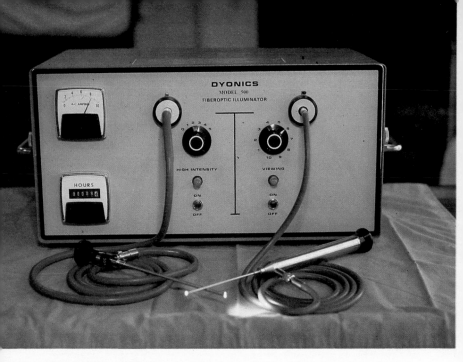

*Above:* Dual light source for the laparoscope. The light controls on the left are for photography, the controls on the right for general examining use. *Below:* Portable light source with laparoscope, cannula, and trochars.

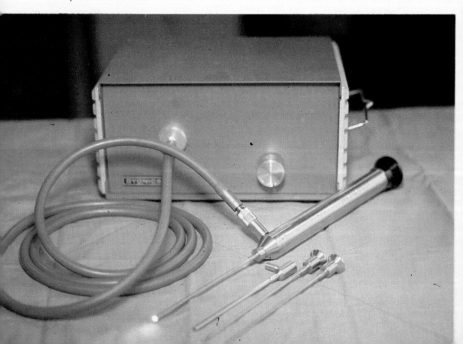

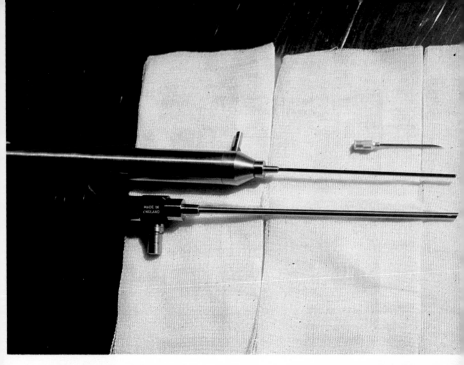

*Above:* Two laparoscopes compared for diameter with a 16-gauge hypodermic needle. *Below:* Laparoscope with attachment for needle biopsy. The biopsy needle enters a special side port of the cannula.

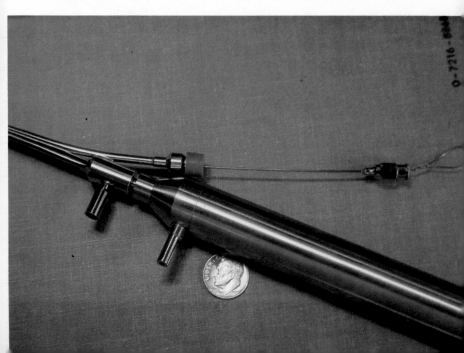

## Why are birds laparoscoped?

Birds are laparoscoped to determine their sex and breeding condition, to examine the internal organs for signs of disease, and to take small tissue samples for microscopic study. In sexually monomorphic species (those in which the male and female show no external differences) laparoscopy is the most common procedure for sex determination. With the world population of all wild animals decreasing rapidly and with federal regulations restricting the importation of many species, captive breeding programs have become increasingly important. Pairing birds of confirmed sex and in good breeding condition can be the most important key to a successful avian propagation program.

## Procedure for sex determination by laparoscopy

For most species, an assistant restrains the bird manually on its right side by holding the wings together over the back and gently extending the legs. If anesthesia is used, a se-

Positioning of a bird is accomplished by holding its wings together over its back and extending its legs slightly posteriorly.

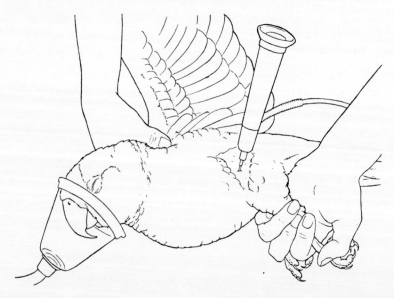

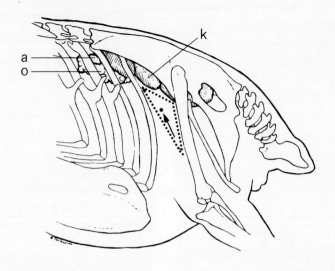

The landmarks for locating the optimum area for introducing the cannula are the last rib, the ilium, and the proximal half of the shaft of the femur. The approximate site is marked by the arrow and dot. *a*, adrenal; *o*, gonad; *k*, kidney.

cond assistant monitors the bird's breathing and heart rate.

A small skin area on the bird's left side is prepared for sterile surgery. The landmarks for locating the optimum area for the procedure are the last rib, the ilium, and the proximal half of the femur. Within the triangle formed by these, a small incision is carefully made through the skin and superficial muscle. This is no more traumatic than giving a hypodermic injection and generally produces no noticeable discomfort to the bird. The hollow sleeve, or *cannula*, containing a sharp pointed rod, the *trochar*, is inserted into the abdominal air sac. The trochar is then removed from the cannula, and the viewing tip of the laparoscope with its light-carrying bundles and optical system is inserted. For birds weighing less than 100 grams, the laparoscope may be inserted directly through the incision without using the cannula, which reduces the diameter of the instrument to 1.7 mm.

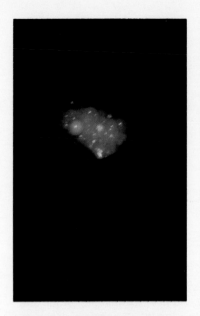
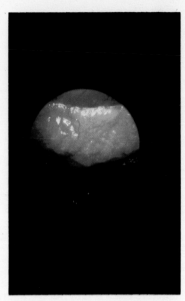

*Above, left:* inactive ovary of an amazon parrot—note undeveloped follicles. *Right:* Immature ovary of a young amazon parrot. *Below, left:* Ovary of a parrot, showing a developing follicle. *Right:* Ovary of a parrot, with a more mature follicle.

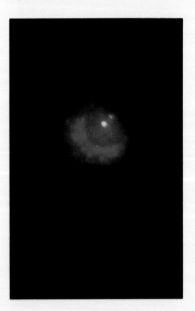

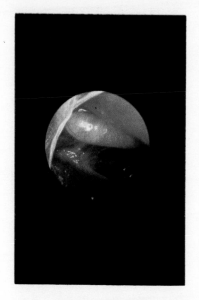

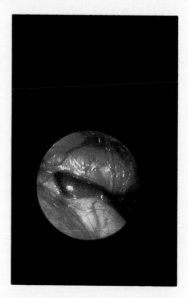

*Above, left:* The white organ in the center is the testicle of a Crowned Crane. *Right:* The dark organ has the normal color of a testicle of a Glossy Ibis. *Below, left:* The white organ in the center is a mature, active testicle of an African Grey Parrot. *Right:* Tuberculosis lesions in the liver of a turaco.

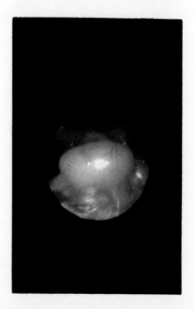

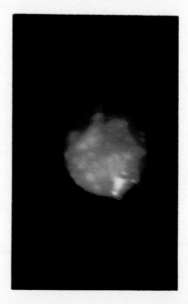

When properly placed, the viewing tip of the laparoscope will be near the anterior (uppermost) lobe of the left kidney, and the gonad will be seen just above this point, attached to the adrenal gland. Identification of the gonad is completed in about one minute, and the laparoscope and cannula are withdrawn. A topical antibiotic powder is placed on the small puncture; sutures are not required.

Whether the examination is done in a veterinary hospital or at an aviary, the laparoscopic equipment is thoroughly cleaned and sterilized before each bird is examined so there is no danger of infection. Liquid or gas sterilization is used since steam-and-heat sterilization is damaging to the lens system of the laparoscope.

## What does the veterinarian see when a bird is laparoscoped?

The ovary in a female bird is a cluster of hundreds of round follicles, each containing an undeveloped ovum. A young bird will have relatively small, uniform follicles. A female bird in breeding condition will show a large developing follicle or a mature follicle just prior to ovulation and egg formation.

The male bird has a smooth, dense testicle, either pale or dark. The veterinarian can evaluate the bird's breeding condition by the size of the testicle and its blood supply. Development and activity of the gonads can be correlated with behavioral data to indicate the bird's response to environmental, nutritional, and husbandry conditions.

## Are there other ways of determining the bird's sex?

In waterfowl and poultry, *vent sexing* remains one of the most useful and rapid techniques for sexing newly hatched young. Many aviculturists effectively utilize this easy-to-learn method. However, there are many other avian species for which this technique is not effective. In these species, aviculturists have paired birds "naturally" by behavioral characteristics. Unfortunately, there is room for error in this method, and many individuals have been paired with another of the same sex.

A modification of the caponizing procedure (*laparotomy*) has been used in various ways to allow direct visualization of the gonads via a small incision and the use of an otoscope or small speculum. This is an effective technique, but it has not gained wide acceptance because size of the surgical incision is relatively large and its application is limited to sexing.

Two nonsurgical techniques for sexing monomorphic birds include *sex chromosome determination* and *fecal steroid analysis*. Both procedures involve a uniquely equipped laboratory and are quite expensive and time consuming. Until recently, fecal steroid laboratory services have been limited primarily to endangered species in large collections, but are now commercially available through local veterinarians in the U.S.

## Are there other uses for avian laparoscopy?

In addition to its use in sex determination, laparoscopy is a versatile diagnostic tool. The air sacs and posterior surface of the lungs may be examined for signs of infection. The kidneys, adrenals, spleen, intestines, and liver may be rapidly evaluated visually, and samples taken for bacteriologic culture or histopathologic study under the microscope. Information about the bird's health is available in a short time without major surgery.

An increasingly common procedure is the liver biopsy. Biopsy results can be of major assistance to the manager of a large or valuable collection that has had a problem with avian tuberculosis, viral hepatitis, amyloidosis, or an inclusion-body disease. This technique can provide rapid and accurate answers about the status of an individual bird without endangering its health, and the manager can use this information to select birds for quarantine or entry into the collection.

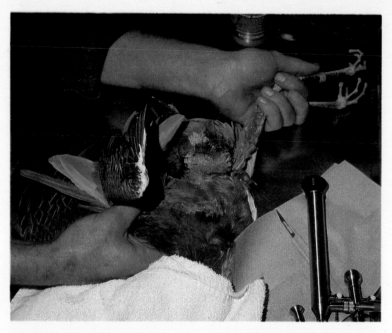

*Above:* A night-heron being prepared for sexing. *Below:* A Nicobar Pigeon is laparoscoped for sex.

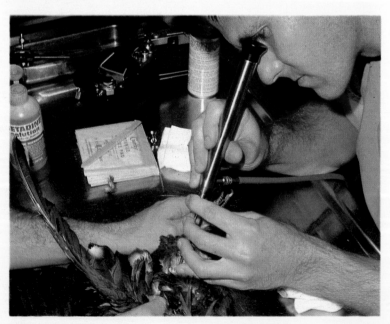

*Right:* An immature night-heron placed on its back for diagnostic liver biopsy to test for avian tuberculosis. *Below, left:* The small piece of tissue in the palm is the sample taken from the liver. *Below, right:* Placement of a single cat-gut suture in the skin of the night-heron after biopsy.

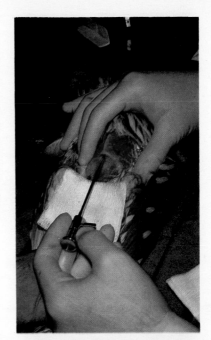

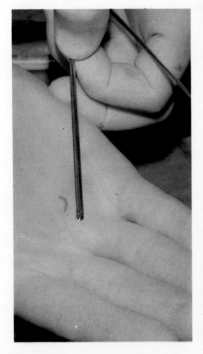

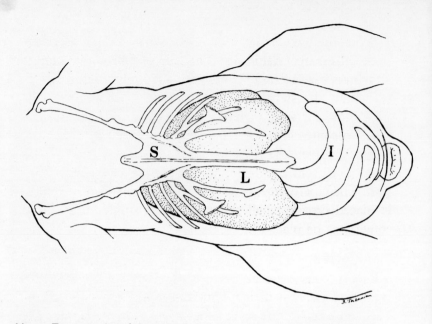

*Above:* Topography of the vental skeleton and superficial viscera. *L,* liver; *S,* sternum; *I,* intestine. *Below:* Lateral topography with the needlescope inserted for examination of the liver.

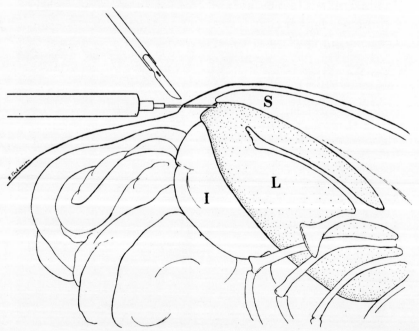

When the liver is to be examined, the bird is placed on its back with its feet held back. The laparoscope with a biopsy attachment is inserted through the abdominal tissue directly behind the sternum in the midline. The surgeon can view most surfaces of the liver and can even examine the heart in some cases. If abnormal tissue is seen on the surface of the liver, the surgeon can take a small portion of this tissue to be sent to the laboratory for microscopic examination. The laparoscope is withdrawn, and a topical antibiotic is placed on the small skin wound. A single suture may sometimes be placed in the skin.

## Conclusion

Laparoscopy, one of the major recent advances in the science of avian medicine, is an important conservation and husbandry technique and diagnostic tool. It is a rapid, safe, noninjurious procedure that allows direct visual observation of the gonads and examination and sampling of the abdominal organs in a living bird. Used as an adjunct to other techniques, laparoscopy has significant applications in the management and conservation of avian species in captivity.

## Supplemental Reading

Bush, M.; Wildt, D. E.; Kennedy, S.; and Seager, S. W. J. 1978. Laparoscopy in zoological medicine. *JAVMA* 173:1081-1087.

Czekala, N. M., and Lasley, B. L. 1977. A technical note on sex determination in monomorphic birds using faecal steroid analysis. *Inter. Zoo Yearbook* 17:209-211.

Harrison, G. J. 1978. Endoscopic examination of avian gonadal tissue. *Vet. Med./Small Animal Clinics* 73:479-484.

McIlwaith, C. W., and Fessler, J. F. 1978. Arthroscopy in the diagnosis of equine joint disease. *JAVMA* 172:263-268.

Satterfield, W. C. 1980. Diagnostic laparoscopy in birds. In *Current Veterinary Therapy VII*, ed. R. W. Kirk. Philadelphia: W. B. Saunders Co.